EVERYTHING IS TEETH

EVIE WYLD

JOE SUMNER

PANTHEON BOOKS
NEW YORK

It's not the images that come first when I think of the parts of my childhood spent in Australia. Or even the people. It's the sounds
— the butcher birds and the magpies that lived amongst us on the back veranda.

And stronger still, the smells —
eucalyptus, watermelon, and filter mud,
rich and rude and sickly strong.

Most of all, the river, muddy and lined with mangrove.

Salt and sulphur;

at low tide the black mud that smelled bad,

that had stingray burrows hollowed out in it.

The smell I associate with the smell of sharks.

At six years old I am bug-eyed, and desperate to know more...

the farmers and fishermen who drop by to see my uncle and grandfather,

and tell me stories about being alone in the water at dusk...

...with something that lurks beneath the surface.

I hassle stories out of my mother. For instance, 'the sand-sifting worm'.

An argument with my father on Heron Island...

He says it's a sand-sifting worm...

she, a deadly sea snake...

While all around them the tide creeps in...

And the people far away on the shore start shouting and waving...

And when it's up to their waists,

they see the small whirlpools in the water...

the fins that flash bronze in the sun...

The weight

beneath the water.

Or I stalk my uncle from behind my mother's legs.

My uncle who reads as a kid that the safest thing to do when a shark comes is to float, pretend to be dead.

knowing that my father hates the water — some leftover phobia from an English public boarding school.

Father Christmas brings my brother a freshly preserved bronze whaler's jaw in a big sack.

I get a punch bag and gloves, as requested.

While everyone else is smoking cigars and eating the Christmas pig, I slide from the table in an awful dress, made by my grandmother. My hair in bunches for the occasion, is not something I'm happy about.

I go to my boxing gloves and check for spiders, then slide them on.

Christmas carries on in the long slow way it does.

And in the evening the grown-ups get drunk, and think it's funny to put their heads through the jaw.

They cut their faces without even knowing.

I find a book...

SHARK ATTACK!

... and I fall in love.

Rodney Fox, I fall for you at six years old.

I see right inside your viscera and you tell me about surviving. I read about how your abdomen was opened

and all your ribs broken. Your diaphragm punctured, lung ripped open, shoulder blade pierced, spleen uncovered.

The tendons in your hand all cut...

The main artery from your heart exposed.

and how the shark left behind a tooth, still stuck in your wrist.

I see the before photograph, impossible red sausages stuffed into an empty carcass, the white skin tender, swollen and peeling away.

And I see the after photograph, the horsehair stitches, that make a perfect semi-circle from shoulder to ribs — a cartoon apple bite.

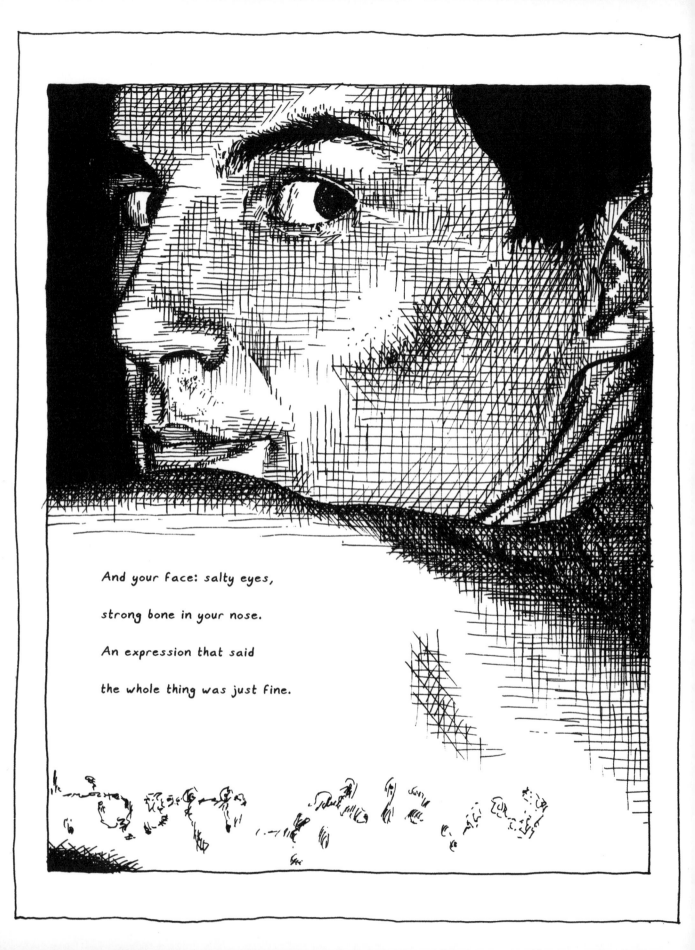

And your face: salty eyes,

strong bone in your nose.

An expression that said

the whole thing was just fine.

Stuck in the mouth, wrestling your thumbs into its eyes till it lets go, and you feel yourself loose in your skin suit.

The shark is gone and people are nudging your guts back inside, and when you wake again it hasn't changed your face. It is all fine.

I solemnly understand you to be the greatest living man.

I make up stories about myself and my schoolmates getting attacked by sharks.

sit in the library scrutinizing the shark books. But this is Sydenham, not Sydney, and there are just two books, thin and hardbacked, with drawings, not photographs, and there are no descriptions of attacks, no mentions of Rodney Fox, just diagrams and graphs. In England they are more interested in whales.

I learn where the spleen is positioned, how deep a tooth would have to go to pierce the diaphragm.

Back home, my brother lingers in doorways with a blank look on his face.

After school he lies on the sofa, flipping through the channels, never letting anyone get more than two sentences out.

There's trouble one night, when it turns out he's been sitting in a café, drinking cola, not going to school at all, not for a long time.

The first time he comes home with a bloody face, my mother cries and I sit stiff, watching her lay sliced cucumber on his swollen eyes, and listening to her swear as she does it.

My brother stays silent and watches a spot not in the room.

That night raised voices come from my parents' room, and my brother comes and lies on the bottom bunk in my room.

My brother coming home with a bruised face or bleeding nose becomes unsurprising. Something makes other people want to hit him, something else makes no-one want to stop him being hit.

My father shouts at the police down the phone, and they can't help. My brother remains silent on the matter, but continues coming into my room and listening to shark stories. Once I start to tell him about a girl at school who'd lost her finger to a rottweiler, but he shakes his head...

Stick to shark stories.

So I tell him about the Mako at Burning Palms that was found with a pair of expensive stilettos in its stomach.

It's the same way with furniture; it's important to be on the bed or sofa – you can't leave your legs dangling like chum. It's too easy to imagine the sofa is a raft.

arrange cushions to stop myself rolling off in a squall, but even so, when I fall asleep they come at me from underneath, turn the raft over with their shovel snouts.

...something waiting to strike.

My father works late and all the time.

My brother watches Jaws, I watch my father and my father looks at his notes.

Looking up now and again between refills.

I like the moustache on Quint, and the beard on Hooper.

Everything about the film seems familiar...

...Brody is scared of the shark...

. Brody's son, Michael, is in hospital for shock after the shark rushes him...

Quint is eaten alive.

I worry about my dog, who hasn't made her mind up about the sofa or the floor.

When Brody explodes the shark, my father looks up from his work and pumps a fist in the air.

Then pours himself another glass of wine to celebrate.

On our next trip back to Australia, I am worried about flying.

I worry the plane will crash.

I'm not scared of it nose-diving into concrete and killing us all instantly...

I'm scared that it will land softly on top of the water, like it does in the safety video, and that we will all be floated out in our life jackets, bright orange with a whistle, to attract attention from above and from below.

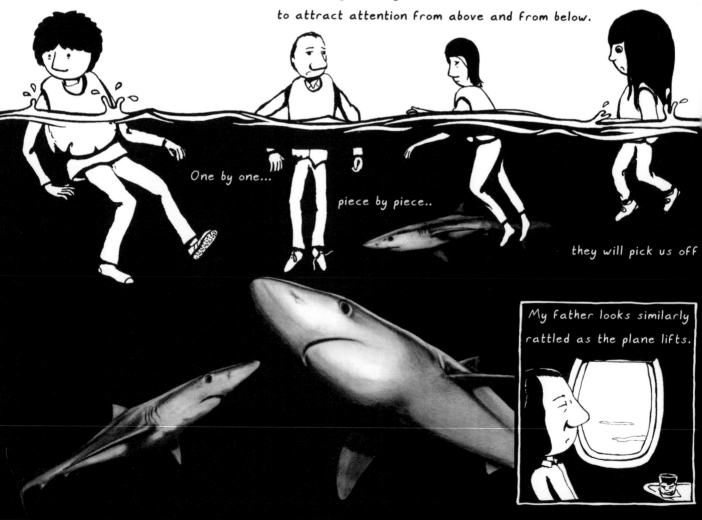

One by one...

piece by piece..

they will pick us off

My father looks similarly rattled as the plane lifts.

He takes two pills and a whisk and sleeps till Singapore

From Sydney we take the small plane to Ballina and arrive at the farm red-nosed and static-haired.

There is a welcome meal of butterfly prawns and mud crab from the river.

There is a large huntsman in our room.

Everything is as it should be.

My mother likes a deserted beach,
but I worry that increases our chances.

I get in up to my knees and the sun turns my hair to hot bread.

I watch my brother up—and—under waves, spurting water like a whale from his mouth each time.

He is far out.

My feet twitch in the sand.

Later, my uncle takes my brother and me to see a dead shark that's been washed up downriver.

We mess with it, my brother sits on it rodeo style. I run a hand over the sandpaper skin I've read about.

Survivors find themselves grazed from it when the shark glides by.

Everything is teeth.

My uncle shows us
the eye trick.

He pokes a finger right in,
and white bone
closes over it.

I think of you, Rodney Fox – did that bone close over your finger?

My mother and I go for night swims in the pool while everyone else is asleep, because I have dreams, and she is awake anyway.

My mother floats on her back and stargazes, and I bob next to her watching for movement in the bottom of the pool.

I wake to find that my mother, brother, cousins and uncle have gone deep-sea fishing without me.

They have deliberately snuck out because there isn't room for me in the boat.

And I am too small to be anything but in the way.

I sulk in the pool for the morning, floating face down

for as long as I can, imagining them coming back and finding me drowned dead from boredom and rejection.

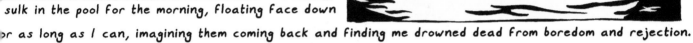

But my father has other plans for the day.

The plan is to drive to Ballina and visit the Giant Prawn. Then on to Lismore for a **surprise**.

Which means a four-hour drive in my uncle's ute, rattling like a pudding cart.

My father and I are not often alone together, and I start to think about my mother at sea,

a capsized boat...

I start to imagine it's

just me and him

from now on.

Ballina's Giant Prawn turns out to be a gas station
with a coach driver's diner where the egg sac should be.

VISIT CONAN!
THE RECORD BREAKING WHITE POINTER!!

I imagine the huge tank inside that must hold Conan the killer shark...

...wonder who Conan has killed,

...d what will happen at feeding time...

...reat hunks of raw meat,

bellowing gops of blood against the bone-white teeth.

And I can't wait.

My father takes a sweaty paw

and we walk through the pointer's chipwood face.

Inside is a mannequin in a boat, dressed in a sou'wester with a mechanism that makes his arm move up and down as he hits a sacking-cloth shark on the nose with his oar.

We are shown into a dark room to see a video.

Vic Hislop shows the fishermen with arms missing...

With legs missing...

With friends missing.

He shows the bite taken out of a tuna.

He puts scary music on.

Vic Hislop drives a fearsome sea cat and strapped to its sides are the carcasses of 16-foot sharks.

He opens up the bellies, tears them apart in public to reveal the squid, the number plates, old boots and crisp packets...

All of which make him laugh.

But the head of a sea lion makes him sober.

I know which one I'd rather see swimming about.

By the end of the video my father's foot is tapping, and I feel sick, but I'm not sure why. He raises his eyebrows at me like Groucho Marx, and we go into the next room, following glow-in-the-dark arrows. I want to get to Conan in his tank, so I can look him in the eye and ask him what he wants.

In the next room, shark jaws.

Photographs too.

Mostly of Vic kneeling next to dead sharks. Always smiling like he's being pictured with an elderly relative.

The room after is about shark attacks, but I've seen all the pictures before.

GREAT WHITE
...M WITH ME
...IS MOUTH

Rodney Fox, you are there, I recognize your spleen, but there are no after photographs with your smiling face.

In the last room is Conan.

He is in a tank but not swimming.

A seventeen—foot white pointer in a tank
maybe seventeen and a half foot long.

Wires shot into his head, back and tail keep him suspended in a liquid the colour of tobacco teeth. Parts of him have flaked away, and his skin has turned from grey blue to brown.

I spy my father that night,
sneaking a smoke at the far end of the veranda, looking for land in the black sea of sugar cane.

He moves his mouth like
he's having an argument
with someone, but no
words come out.

Inside, a yellow lampshade colours the sound of
everyone else at dinner.

Someone sings a rude song.

What follows

is a humiliating trip to the doctor, who, in trying to get a smile out of me, suggests weeing on the stings.

I stare at him in silence, wondering
if he will use his own urine.

In the end he gives us some cream, instructions not to go in the sea for a week, and a badge...

I've
been to
see the
Doctor

...which I lose in the car park in case anybody asks me why I've been to see the doctor.

The things
underneath the water didn't want me there.

I still follow my mother and brother to the beach and stand in the shallows.

My mother never goes out past the breakers, except this once, because she has turned forty.

She strides out with my brother and catches a big wave in, her mouth a big rectangle of smile.

From the shore I can see how it would happen: the legs torn off,

the stubby nose in the guts, the fingers all sliced away.

She'll do it again at fifty.

My brother stays out there floating, dangling.

He's told me he often sees dark shapes darting out of the corner of his eye, but they are porpoise.

'Sharks don't come around when porpoise are there,' he tells me.

eah, except when they want to eat the porpoise.

On the day when the barometer breaks,
we all go out together to pull up the shark line.

My mother fishes for flathead out the back, while my
brother lies belly down on the prow of the boat,
trailing a hand in the water, making my father bark.

My father is dangerously hot, having
dressed against the elements.

Woollen socks tucked into trousers
keep out mosquitoes.

Thick white sunscreen on the naked flesh of his
face between sunglasses, peaked hat
and upturned collar ensure an
impregnable barrier against the sun.

My uncle heaves up a live seven-footer who shakes her head at him, more alive than the rest.

The tinny—sluggish, sharks inside and out—drags itself towards shore.

Looking over the side at the white belly, or the black eye as the shark twists against the motor, I can't help thinking...

IF SHE JUST WENT UNDER THE BOAT SHE COULD TURN US OUT.

But she doesn't and is hauled up into the mangrove and
left to thrash and
wear herself out and die.

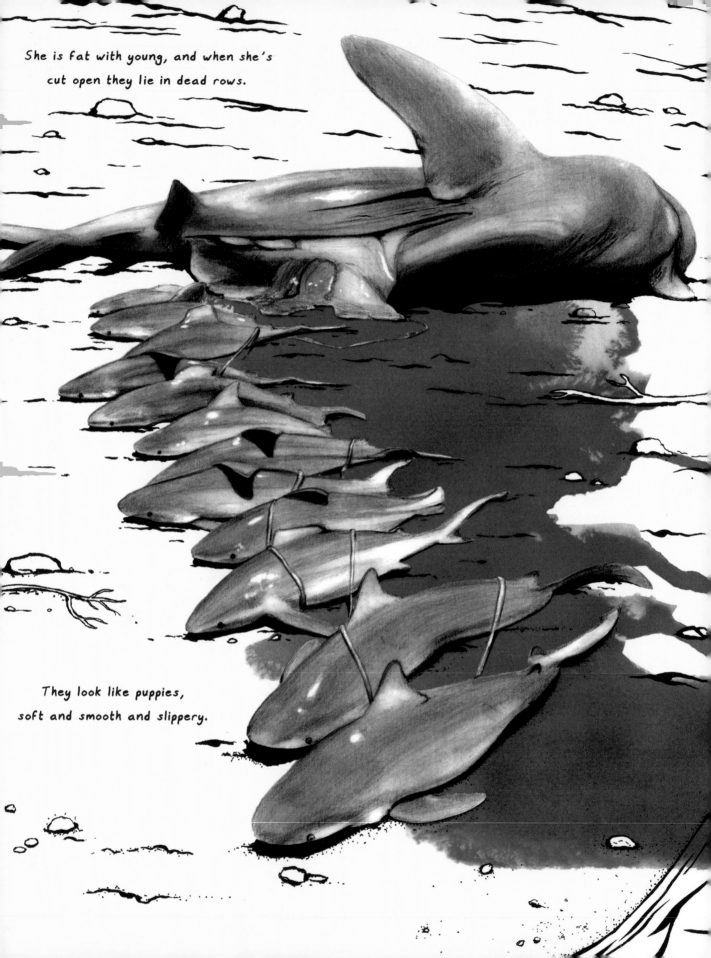

She is fat with young, and when she's
cut open they lie in dead rows.

They look like puppies,
soft and smooth and slippery.

I get one to hold and watch as my uncle cuts out the mother's mouth, then saws off her fins and rolls the trunk back into the river.

We take two puppies back home for frying.

I feel worse than when, in order to accommodate the new microwave, the pet goldfish were poured into Peckham Rye pond.

Along with crisp packets, cans of Rio, the odd pair of trousers.

My parents went deep-sea fishing a long time before I was born.

They caught parrot fish and snapper, trevally and coral-cod.

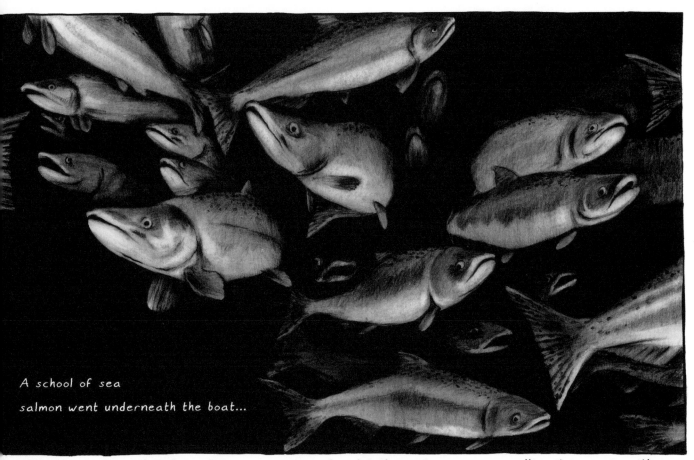

A school of sea
salmon went underneath the boat...

The sea broke with fish, and as soon as your line hit the water you were pulling it in again with a huge one hooked.

As quickly as it started, it stopped

and everyone watched mutely

as a tiger shark,

pale blue and clean,

bigger than the boat,

passed under,

its fin skimming the hull.

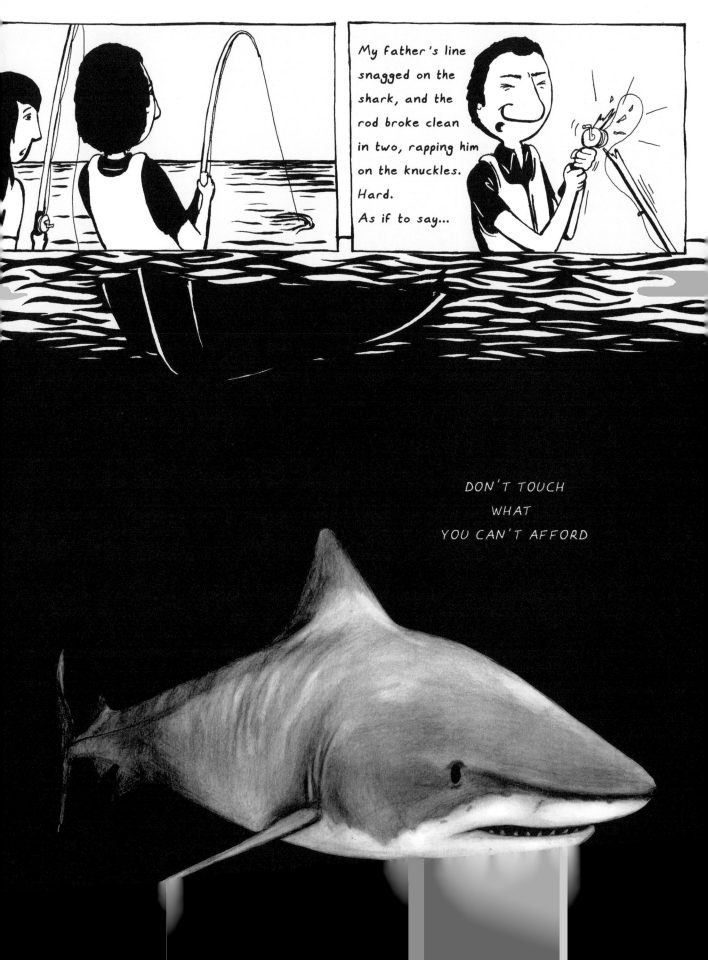

When my week of no swimming is up, I'm unsure about the water again. The salt chews on my stings, but it's hot so I sit in the shallows watching my mother on her back, not far away.

If I think the worst, then the worst is unlikely to happen.

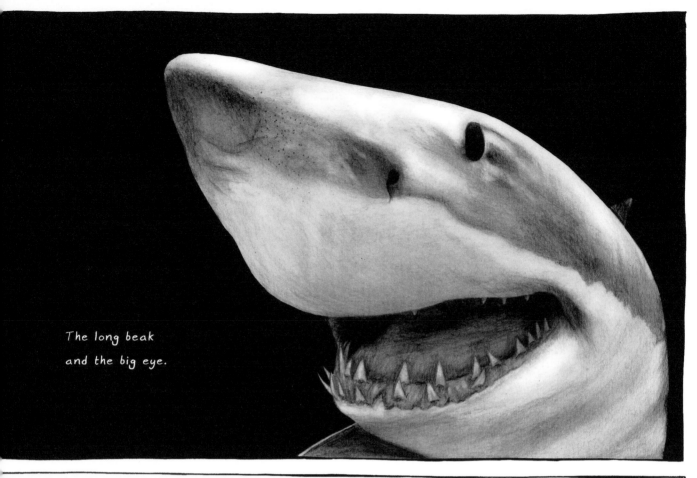

The long beak
and the big eye.

The slow rolling...   the great white belly up and catching the sun, the clean, the smooth, the flash and the bump.

Later, when my mother comes in,
I think, 'Two nil to us.'

As she dries in the sun, we watch my brother far out lying on his board.

The worst can't happen —

a white pointer, breaching,

takes him down like a sea lion.

A red streak and a broken board, and nothing much else is left.

The pointer turns, my brother's leg sticking out of her mouth.

She comes for my mother,

takes her from the hip as she grasps the only bit left of her son.

He puts an arm around my mother's shoulders
and laughs at her for worrying.

He has become
a head taller than her.

A lot changes with time...

I know now that Rodney's shark
wasn't trying to murder him.

Her thoughts were

only of the fish Fox

had tied to his

weight belt.

Benign, indifferent and essential, she passed through his life,
     and left an open hole in her wake.

Rodney Fox fought her on his own terms...

An inhalation of breath.

In memory of Andrew, Gladys, Phil,
Quint and Speedy.

And in celebration of Rodney Fox
and the Shark Attack Survivors for Shark Conservation

All rights reserved. Published in the United States by Pantheon Books,

a division of Penguin Random House LLC, New York.

Originally published in hardcover in Great Britain by Jonathan Cape,

an imprint of Vintage Publishing, a division of Penguin Random House Ltd., London, in 2015.

Pantheon Books and colophon are registered trademarks of Penguin Random House LLC.

Library of Congress Cataloging-in-Publication Data

Wyld, Evie.

Everything is teeth / Evie Wyld ; illustrated by Joe Sumner.

pages ; cm

ISBN 978-1-101-87081-5 (hardcover : alk. paper). ISBN 978-1-101-87082-2 (eBook).

1. Wyld, Evie—Comic books, strips, etc. 2. Sharks—Comic books, strips, etc. 3. Women authors,

English—Biography. 4. Australia-New South Wales—Comic books, strips, etc. 5. Graphic novels.

I. Sumner, Joe, illustrator. II. Title.

PR6123.Y43Z46 2016   823'.92-dc23   (B)   2015023575

www.pantheonbooks.com

Cover illustrations by Joe Sumner

Cover design by Kelly Blair

Printed in China

First United States Edition

2 4 6 8 9 7 5 3 1